D0504343

LOOK INSIDE

A GREEK THEATRE

PETER CHRISP
Illustrated by Adam Hook

WAYLAND

Editor: Jason Hook
Designer: Danny McBride

First published in 2000 by Wayland Publishers Ltd,
61 Western Road, Hove, East Sussex BN3 1JD, England
© Copyright 2000 Wayland Publishers Ltd
Find Wayland on the Internet at http://www.wayland.co.uk

British Library Cataloguing in Publication Data
Chrisp, Peter
    A Greek theatre. - (Look inside)
    1. Theatre - Greece - History - To 500 2. Greece - Social
life and customs - Juvenile literature 3. Greece -
Civilization - To 146 B.C. - Juvenile literature
    I. Title II. Hook, Adam
    792'.0938

ISBN 0 7502 2589 0

Cover pictures: Vase painting of a Greek comedy (centre);
a statuette of a comic actor (top); a tragic mask (bottom-
left); the winning playwright's ivy wreath (bottom-right).
Ivy wreath constructed by Peter Chrisp.

Picture Acknowledgements: The publishers would like to
thank the following for permission to publish their pictures:
(t=top; c=centre; b=bottom; l=left; r=right) AKG London
cover (t), 25b; AKG London /Erich Lessing 5r, 6b, 8t, 9bl, 11b,
16b, 21t, 23t; AKG Berlin 11t; Ancient Art & Architecture
Collection cover (bl), 4t, 9cr, 20t, 22t, 24t, 26br; Bridgeman
Art Library /Louvre /Peter Willi 12–13, /Louvre 17b, /Museo
Archeologico Nazionale 12l, /Ashmolean Museum 13b,
/Hermitage, Russia 26t; C M Dixon 14b, 16t; e.t. archive 10b,
18, 22b, 26bl; Robert Harding Picture Library /Tony Gervis 5l;
Michael Holford cover (c), 4b, 14t, 17t, 19t, 21b, 23bl, 24b,
28b, 29; Numismatic Museum, Athens 9t; Stockmarket Photo
Agency /Larry Lefever 6t; Trustees of the British Museum 7t,
10t, 27t; Wayland Picture Library 15, 23br, 27b, /Zul
Mukhida/Peter Chrisp cover (br), 28t; Werner Forman
Archive 19b, /Museo Gregoriano Profano, The Vatican, Rome
25t.

Production Controller: Carol Titchener
Printed and bound by G. Canale & C.S.p.A, Turin, Italy
Colour reproduction by Page Turn, Hove, England

All artwork is by Adam Hook. All quotes are credited on page 31.

AULOS 16

PIGLET 6

BIRD COSTUME 14

CONTENTS

THEATRE

THE ORCHESTRA

Take a look inside a Greek theatre. You take your place in one of the curving rows of seats, which rise up the hillside. Far below, you see the circular *orchestra*, or dancing floor, with a small building behind it called the *skene*. In front of the skene, two comic actors are carefully rehearsing their performance.

▶ Paintings on vases show us what Greek plays looked like. These two comic actors wear padded costumes and magnificent masks.

It was the ancient Greeks who invented drama, more than 2,500 years ago. The first plays in the Western world were staged at Athens, in around 500 BC. They were performed in the theatre shown on the left. Plays continued to be performed here for almost 800 years.

This theatre was rebuilt several times and almost nothing remains of the earliest building. The skene, where the actors changed their costumes, disappeared a long time ago. Used as a backdrop to the play, the skene was decorated to look like a palace, street or cave.

◀ The orchestra of the theatre at Athens. Originally it was completely round.

Greek theatres could hold audiences of up to 20,000 people. They were cleverly designed to make sounds carry a long way, so that everyone could hear the actors. At the ancient theatre in Epidaurus, you can sit in the back row and still hear a coin dropped in the orchestra.

COMEDIES
by Aristophanes
of Athens,
Son of Philippus

'FESTIVAL TIME
SCENE: A street in Athens.' 1
[Look on page 31 to find where our quotes are from.]

▼ The theatre at Epidaurus. The seated area was called the *theatron*, or viewing place.

▼ Actors wore big masks with exaggerated features which the whole audience could see.

'The actor Callipides was called "the ape" because he overacted so grossly.' 2

A special type of acting was required in the enormous theatres. The actors wore masks, partly because most people in the audience were too far away to see any changes of expression. To show their feelings, actors made grand gestures with their arms and bodies.

Many features of Greek theatre, such as the use of masks, seem strange to us. But much of what we know of the theatre came from the Greeks. Many theatrical words are Greek, including drama, actor, scene, comedy and tragedy. The word theatre itself comes from *theatron*, the Greek word for the area where the audience sat.

PIGLET

FESTIVAL OF DIONYSUS

As the sun rises, a priest walks solemnly towards the altar in the centre of the orchestra. He is holding a piglet, which wriggles and squeals in his arms. The piglet will be sacrificed at the altar – killed and burnt as an offering to the god Dionysus.

▶ A piglet had to be sacrificed at the theatre before the plays could begin.

'O Lord Dionysus,
Accept with favour this offering
and this procession,
As we honour you at your festival.' [3]

Greek plays were always performed as part of religious festivals, to honour the gods. Usually, they were performed for Dionysus, who was the god of drama. In Athens, there was a festival procession for Dionysus. A man in the costume and mask of the god was pulled through the streets in a cart built to look like a ship.

▼ An Athenian man dressed as Dionysus with his ship and his followers called *satyrs*, who had the ears and tails of horses.

Dionysus was also god of spring, when festivals were held in his honour. The Greeks believed Dionysus sailed across the sea each spring, bringing fine weather. His procession reminded people that it was the start of the sailing season. After the winter storms, ships could once more sail in safety.

'Come to Athens,
home of the brave,
Blessed with festivals
through all the year;
And in spring,
for Dionysus,
A festival of
singing, dancing,
And the whistle and
throb of pipes.' 4

◀ This painting on a vase shows Dionysus as the god of wine.

On vase paintings, Dionysus often holds a drinking vessel and long, trailing grapevines, which show that he was also the god of wine. Each spring in Greece, the previous year's wine harvest, which had been stored in pots all winter, was ready for drinking. So the festival of Dionysus was also a celebration of wine.

As god of wine, which makes people drunk and out of control, Dionysus was also worshipped as god of wild behaviour. In stories, he was often followed by crazed women called maenads. These women left their homes, then danced and ran through the woods in a wild frenzy. They ripped apart animals with their bare hands, and ate them raw.

'On, on! Run and dance!
Sing to the rattle of thunderous drums!
Sing for joy!
Praise Dionysus, god of joy!' 5

▲ Maenads tear a deer in two.

TOKEN

THE AUDIENCE

In the early morning, the audience pay their tokens and make their way into the theatre. Two ambassadors from Sparta, wearing scarlet cloaks, sit down on marble seats in the front row. They have never been to a play before, as there is no theatre in Sparta. They are suspicious, but also curious about what the day will hold.

▲ Beautifully decorated marble seats were reserved for priests and important officials.

▼ Long hair and scarlet cloaks show that these two spectators are visitors from Sparta.

The ancient Greeks never belonged to a single nation or state. Every Greek city was like a little state, with its own government. There were hundreds of rival city-states, the two most powerful being Athens and Sparta.

In spring, when the theatre festival was held, Athens was full of visitors taking advantage of the start of the sailing season. Merchants and ambassadors arrived from all the other cities. Important visitors were welcomed to the theatre, and given the best seats. The Athenians were proud of their city and its festival. They enjoyed the chance to show off their artistic skills in front of fellow Greeks.

◀ Theatre tokens, decorated with actors' masks.

Beautiful lead 'entry tokens' have been found at ancient sites. Most members of the audience paid a small entrance fee, which raised funds for the upkeep of the theatre. There was also a state fund which allowed the poorest citizens to get free seats.

'Comedy's tough and the audience is tougher.
Your praise is like blossom in the spring:
very nice while it lasts.
Need I mention the treatment you gave poor old Crates?
The hisses? The boos?' 6

'There's a sensible crowd in today – all except one.
No don't moan!
We're talking about Cleophon, The windbag over there.' 7

Experts believe that women did not go to the theatre. The plays were written and performed by men, for a male audience. These men were often noisy and excited. They showed what they thought of the plays by heckling, hissing, whistling, hooting, cheering and kicking their heels. A sad scene could make them weep.

▲ A jug decorated with a comic actor's mask.

◀ Women's roles were performed by men – another reason for wearing masks.

The dramatic festival at Athens proved so popular that other Greek cities began to build theatres too. The theatre's popularity in ancient Greece is shown by the many household objects decorated with actors' masks which have been found all over the Greek world.

9

PAPYRUS ROLL

POEMS AND PLAYS

The poet and playwright Euripides sits at his table. He is adding the finishing touches to his latest play, *The Women of Troy*. It is based on an old story by Homer, the most famous Greek poet. Euripides dips his reed pen into the ink, and writes down the final lines.

'My father wanted to make a good man of me, and made me learn off the whole of Homer. Homer, with his supreme wisdom, has written about almost every human activity.'[8]

▲ Plays were written on paper made from papyrus, an Egyptian marsh plant.

Homer is thought to have lived in the eighth century BC, some 300 years before the time of Euripides. The Greeks knew little about Homer's life, but they loved his two long poems, *The Iliad* and *The Odyssey*. He was so important to the ancient Greeks that he was referred to simply as 'The Poet'.

In his stories, Homer retold myths which were already old in his time. His tales of legendary Greek heroes, such as Achilles and Odysseus, provided the perfect plots and characters for playwrights to use.

◀ A bust of the poet Homer. It is believed that he was blind.

Euripides was a playwright who specialized in 'tragedies'. These were serious plays about the sufferings of a great hero or heroine, almost always based on a myth. His greatest rivals were Aeschylus and Sophocles. Between them, they wrote almost 300 plays, of which just thirty-three survive. Other playwrights also wrote tragedies, but their works have all been lost.

▶ The playwright Euripides receives a mask, in front of a statue of Dionysus.

'The sad stories of great men last longer than of humble folk.' 10

'My plays are stuffed full of Homer. Look at my characters: Teucer, Patroclus, Men eager to leap into battle, Great-hearted heroes the audience could learn from.' 9

Homer's stories were not the only ones used by playwrights. Every city had its own legends. In Athens, many stories were told of the local hero Theseus, who was a famous killer of monsters.

Everybody knew the stories, but different playwrights treated the same story in very different ways. In one play, Theseus might be shown as a noble hero. In another, he could be cold-hearted and selfish.

◀ The hero Theseus, here fighting a giant, was the subject of three plays by Euripides.

PROTAGONIST

ACTORS

In the skene building, the *protagonist*, or main actor, is pulling on a costume made from goatskin. Today, he is playing Silenus, leader of the satyrs. The actor gazes at his mask, with its white beard and crown of ivy. In a moment, he will have to become this old man.

◄ A comic actor masked and padded to play the role of a woman.

▼ With a quick costume change, the same actor could play a man.

▼ An actor checks his mask as he prepares to play Silenus, leader of the satyrs.

'When he tried to play the heroes who fought at Troy, you drove him from the stage with hisses and catcalls, and came near to pelting him with stones.' 11

Acting in an ancient Greek play was very demanding work. The actors were professionals. They spent years studying their art, learning how to use their voices and bodies to successfully play different roles.

There were usually only three actors in a play. These were the protagonist, who played the main role, and the second and third *agonists*, who played everyone else. Since they used masks, the actors could make quick changes of character. An actor might rush off stage as an old man, and return a moment later as a young slave girl.

In the early fifth century, each playwright had a favourite actor who he always used as his protagonist. Sophocles, for example, wrote his leading parts for an actor called Tlepolemus.

By the end of the century, the actors for each play were chosen by drawing lots. This was because plays were put on in competition. People realized it gave a playwright an advantage if he always had the best actor.

◄ Pottery figures of actors are often found in Greek graves.

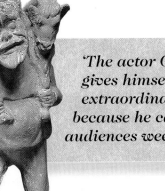

'The actor Callipides gives himself extraordinary airs because he can set vast audiences weeping.' 13

◄ A comic actor dressed to play the part of a goatherd.

The best protagonists became famous. They had the power to turn a poor play into a big hit with the audience. A bad protagonist, though, could ruin a masterpiece with his poor performance.

Masks served as 'sound boxes', making an actor's voice vibrate when he cried out. In tragedies, actors frequently wailed and moaned. Vibrations caused by their masks could turn such cries into powerful sound effects.

▶ Pottery statuettes of comic actors may have been souvenirs of a visit to the theatre.

BIRD COSTUME

CHORUS

A group of men in feathered costumes dance and whirl into the orchestra, flapping their arms and doing their best to imitate the movements of birds. As the audience cheers, they sing together: 'There's nothing better than a pair of wings!' They are the chorus, whose singing and dancing are an important part of the play.

▲ A member of the bird chorus.

▼ The actors in this chorus are playing the part of clouds who have taken the shape of women.

'We're the clouds.
We do you more good
than all the other gods.
But if you misbehave,
we send thunder,
drizzle and hail.' 14

Every Greek play had a chorus of men who danced, sang songs and spoke as a group. In tragedies, the chorus had twelve or fifteen members. They played ordinary people, while the actors played kings, queens or gods. In comedies there was a chorus of twenty-eight members, who played creatures such as ostriches, dolphins, wasps or frogs. In one comedy, the chorus actors even played clouds.

◀ This chorus had to do a piggy-back dance during a play.

'There's nothing better than a pair of wings! If you had wings – yes you, or you – And you suddenly felt hungry sitting there, You could flap off home, Fix yourself a bite to eat, and swoop right back.' 15

Unlike the professional actors, the chorus were ordinary citizens. They spent weeks before the festival learning their songs and dances, with a musician and a trainer. Their training and costumes were paid for by a rich citizen called a *choregos*. He was also expected to provide a feast for the chorus members after the play finished.

'As for Antimachus, meanest of men, Our former choregos, He sent us away without any supper at all!' 16

In a tragedy, the chorus often questioned the hero or heroine, asking them to explain their awful behaviour. The chorus also helped to explain the action to the audience. At the end of the play, they provided a moral like the one below.

'Gods bring many matters to surprising ends. The things we thought would happen did not happen. And that is what has happened here today.' 17

▲ Members of a Greek chorus dressed as warriors riding ostriches.

MUSIC

Two clear, piercing notes ring out, and echo around the theatre. A musician strides into the orchestra, his cheeks swelling as he blows through his *aulos*, or double-pipes. Moving his fingers with speed and skill, he starts to play a fast, rhythmic melody to which the chorus begins to dance.

'Bad aulos players hurl themselves about as if they were pretending to throw a discus.' [18]

▲ The aulos player dances while he plays for the chorus.

Music and dance were just as important as the words in Greek theatre. The lines were sometimes sung or just spoken to a musical accompaniment. An ancient Greek play must have been like a cross between an opera, a ballet and a modern play.

◄ The aulos was the most popular Greek musical instrument, especially to accompany dancers.

The aulos had a vibrating reed, like a clarinet or an oboe, and sound-holes like a recorder. A cloth band worn around the player's face supported his cheeks, helping him to blow. The aulos was played in the theatre, at dinner parties and for religious processions.

◀ The god Apollo plays a *kithara*, or box-lyre.

Greek musicians also played the *lyre*, which was like a small harp. A *kithara*, or box-lyre, was often played by the actors in the theatre.

Played offstage, a lyre could provide sound effects. In Sophocles' satyr play *The Trackers*, the god Hermes invents the first lyre. When it is played, the cowardly satyrs fall flat on their faces, terrified at the strange new sound.

'Euripides was teaching the chorus a part set to a serious tune, when one of them unexpectedly started laughing. "Sir," said Euripides, "you must be very stupid indeed if you can laugh while I sing in the grave mixed Lydian mode."' [20]

Different modes or styles of music were used in plays to create different atmospheres. For sad scenes, playwrights chose a gloomy style called the 'mixed Lydian mode'.

▶ Dionysus with his maenads, who dance to the aulos.

FLYING MACHINE

STAGE EFFECTS

From offstage a comic actor cries: 'Gee up Pegasus!' Behind the skene building, stagehands pull on the ropes that operate the flying machine. There are gasps from the audience, followed by laughter and applause. The actor flies into view, riding through the air on the back of an enormous dung-beetle!

▶ The hero of Aristophanes' play *Peace* flies over the stage on a model of a huge dung-beetle.

The 'flying machine' was a wooden crane, mounted on the roof of the skene building. Euripides often used it to end his tragedies, with gods flying down from the sky. In one play, he showed the hero Bellerophon attempting to ride to heaven on the back of a winged horse called Pegasus, a famous creature from myths.

Aristophanes loved making fun of Euripides' use of stage effects. His hero also tries to fly to heaven, but instead of riding on a winged horse he flies on a dung-beetle. A flying horse needs hay, but a dung-beetle eats dung, so he only has to go to the toilet to feed his mount! The prop-makers must have had fun constructing the huge beetle from wood.

◀ Bellerophon flying on his winged horse Pegasus.

Special effects were an important part of the Greek theatre. Pebbles were poured into bronze vessels to make the sound of thunder. Euripides also liked using an effect called the *eccyclema* or 'roll-out'. This was a trolley, which could be wheeled out of the skene door.

▲ A scene from Euripides' *Alcmene*.

The eccyclema was often used to move dead characters on to the stage. In a play called *Alcmene*, Euripides showed a jealous husband trying to burn his wife on an altar. The altar could also have been rolled out using the eccyclema.

'DIKAIOPOLIS: *Come out Euripides!*
EURIPIDES: *I'm too busy!*
DIKAIOPOLIS: *Use the eccyclema!*
Have yourself rolled out, like you always do.' 22

At one Greek theatre, in Eretria, a tunnel has been found leading from the skene building to the centre of the orchestra. This was used by actors playing ghosts and underworld gods. They made surprise appearances in front of the audience, as if they had just risen from the land of the dead. The tunnel was called 'Charon's Steps', after the ferryman who rowed the dead to the underworld.

▲ Greek actors playing ghosts once crawled through this tunnel in Eretria.

TRAGIC MASK

Tragedy

The audience gasps in horror as the actor playing Oedipus staggers out of the skene door. Blood flows from the eye-sockets of his mask. Oedipus has discovered something terrible about his own past. He finds this knowledge so unbearable that he has just torn out his own eyes.

▲ This mask was worn by an actor playing a tragic king such as Oedipus.

'CHORUS: Horror beyond all bearing! How could you do this?
OEDIPUS: Why should I have eyes when all I saw was ugly? I am lost, hated by the gods, no man so damned!' [23]

Sophocles' tragedy, *King Oedipus*, tells the story of a man who grows up not knowing his true identity. Oedipus kills his father and marries his mother, without realizing who they are. When he discovers what he has done, Oedipus blinds himself.

'The CHORUS: Look! Here was Oedipus, greatest of men, envied by all. See what a sea of misfortunes swept over his head. Let no man be called happy until he carries his happiness down to the grave.' [24]

◀ The blinded Oedipus walks towards the audience.

Special effects were an important part of the Greek theatre. Pebbles were poured into bronze vessels to make the sound of thunder. Euripides also liked using an effect called the *eccyclema* or 'roll-out'. This was a trolley, which could be wheeled out of the skene door.

The eccyclema was often used to move dead characters on to the stage. In a play called *Alcmene*, Euripides showed a jealous husband trying to burn his wife on an altar. The altar could also have been rolled out using the eccyclema.

'*DIKAIOPOLIS: Come out Euripides!*
EURIPIDES: I'm too busy!
DIKAIOPOLIS: Use the eccyclema!
Have yourself rolled out, like you always do.' 22

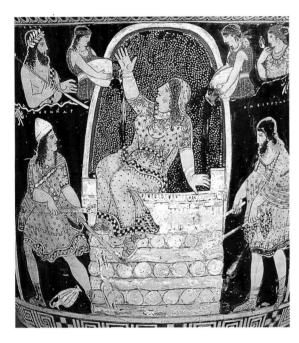

▲ A scene from Euripides' *Alcmene*.

At one Greek theatre, in Eretria, a tunnel has been found leading from the skene building to the centre of the orchestra. This was used by actors playing ghosts and underworld gods. They made surprise appearances in front of the audience, as if they had just risen from the land of the dead. The tunnel was called 'Charon's Steps', after the ferryman who rowed the dead to the underworld.

▲ Greek actors playing ghosts once crawled through this tunnel in Eretria.

TRAGIC MASK

TRAGEDY

The audience gasps in horror as the actor playing Oedipus staggers out of the skene door. Blood flows from the eye-sockets of his mask. Oedipus has discovered something terrible about his own past. He finds this knowledge so unbearable that he has just torn out his own eyes.

▲ This mask was worn by an actor playing a tragic king such as Oedipus.

'CHORUS: *Horror beyond all bearing! How could you do this?*
OEDIPUS: *Why should I have eyes when all I saw was ugly? I am lost, hated by the gods, no man so damned!*' [23]

Sophocles' tragedy, *King Oedipus*, tells the story of a man who grows up not knowing his true identity. Oedipus kills his father and marries his mother, without realizing who they are. When he discovers what he has done, Oedipus blinds himself.

'The CHORUS: *Look! Here was Oedipus, greatest of men, envied by all. See what a sea of misfortunes swept over his head. Let no man be called happy until he carries his happiness down to the grave.*' [24]

◀ The blinded Oedipus walks towards the audience.

Greek tragedies show how people behave in terrible situations. Sons kill mothers, mothers kill children, and wives kill husbands. This allows the audience to face their worst nightmares, in the safety of the theatre.

'Teaching, instruction, the job of the poet. That's what we've always done. Children have teachers to teach them. And grown-ups have playwrights, to set good examples.' 25

◄ An actor gazes at his mask as he prepares to play the part of a tragic heroine.

Tragic playwrights were seen as teachers. They made their audience think about the most important questions of life, such as 'Why do we suffer?'. By raising such questions, tragedies were thought to make the people who watched them into better citizens.

Tragedies were performed for three days during the festival. On each day, a different playwright put on four plays – three tragedies followed by a light-hearted play with a chorus of satyrs. At the end of the festival, a prize was awarded to the author of the best plays.

Sophocles was the most successful writer of tragedies. In his long career, which lasted sixty-two years, Sophocles' plays always won first or second prize at their festivals.

▶ Sophocles wrote more than 120 plays for theatre festivals.

SATYR PLAYS

It is late afternoon. Members of the audience look pale and exhausted, after sitting through the horrors of three tragedies in a row. It is time for the satyr play. A group of men wearing horses' tails dance out into the orchestra. Now there will be some fun!

'Oh to be really drunk! A man is mad
Who won't get drunk when drink is to be had.
If I were drunk –
Oh how I'd chase the girls!' [26]

◀ A horse's tail bobbed behind each satyr as he danced.

▼ This vase from Athens shows three satyrs enjoying a celebration.

Like tragedies, the satyr plays used plots taken from myths. But a satyr play treated these stories in a light-hearted way. There was always a chorus of satyrs, which were men with the ears and tail of a horse.

Plots in satyr plays are often about the wonderful gifts given to humans by the gods. These include the invention of the lyre by Hermes; Dionysus creating wine; and Prometheus bringing the first fire to earth.

Jokes are made about the way the satyrs react to the gods' gifts. When a satyr sees fire for the first time, he thinks it is so pretty that he tries to kiss it. Prometheus warns him, 'You silly goat! You'll singe your beard!'

◀ Dionysus, the leader of the satyrs, sailing past dolphins in a ship with a mast of vines.

'Bring us enjoyment,
Sweet laughter
and song,
Wine, dancing
and pleasure,
All festival long.' 27

The plays show satyrs as foolish creatures, who are interested only in pleasure. They are followers of Dionysus, and like to spend all their time drinking wine and dancing. For the satyrs, life is just one long party.

Satyrs are also terrible cowards. In Euripides' *The Cyclops*, the hero Odysseus is imprisoned by a one-eyed giant, who has threatened to eat him. In return for wine, the satyrs promise to help Odysseus blind the giant. But when the moment comes, they invent ridiculous excuses.

The satyrs' excuses for not fighting a giant:
'We're too far away to reach his eye.'
'And just this moment we've gone lame.'
'We sprained our ankles, I don't know how.' 28

▶ A bowl for mixing wine with water.

Odysseus is able to blind the giant by first getting him drunk. Wine appears again and again in satyr plays. This reminded the theatre audience of Dionysus, the god of wine whose festival they were celebrating.

◀ Odysseus blinds the one-eyed giant.

COMIC MASK

COMEDY

L oud bangs, crashes and shouts come from the skene building. The door flies open and an actor is hurled out, doing a somersault. His ragged costume and ugly mask show that he is playing a slave. Sitting up, he brushes the dust off his huge padded belly, looks at the audience, and says: 'My master's in a bad mood today!'

▶ A flask from 150 BC showing an actor talking to his audience. Look at the amazing mouth of his mask.

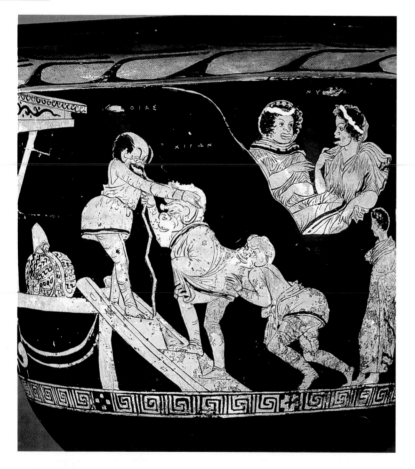

▲ Two comic slaves help their sick old master climb up a set of steps.

Five playwrights each put on a comedy on the last day of the festival. The first great comic playwright was Aristophanes. He loved making up fantastic plots. His plays were like strange dreams in which anything might happen.

Aristophanes wanted to make people laugh, but he also used his jokes to make serious points. His plays often made fun of leading Athenians in the audience, and suggested how they could improve the way they ran the city.

'It's time to break into the play
With some serious moments,
and give you some advice.' 29

After Aristophanes' death, a style called 'New Comedy' became popular. The leading writer was called Menander. Instead of mocking famous Athenians, Menander made fun of everyday 'types', such as mean old men, foolish youths and cunning slaves. He wrote about ordinary life – especially love affairs.

'Aristophanes, prince of comedians: Is your author tonight. All the others are second-rate, With their feeble jokes about rags and lice, and runaway slaves.' 30

◀ Menander with the masks used for the New Comedy.

▼ In New Comedy, costumes were less padded.

'O Menander! O Life! I wonder which of you has copied which?' 31

Aristophanes' comedies were written for a local audience, who understood all the jokes about Athens. But Menander's comedies could be understood by anyone, so he had a much wider appeal. For hundreds of years, Menander's plays were performed in Greek and Roman theatres. His influence is still with us, in modern farces and comedies.

'Why should an educated man go to the theatre, except to enjoy Menander?' 32

▲ Slave characters in New Comedy plays still wore grotesque masks.

ARMOUR

WAR AND POLITICS

An actor dressed in armour rushes forward. The audience recognizes the gorgon which decorates his shield and armour. This character is Lamachus, one of Athens' leading generals. He roars: 'We, Lord Lamachus, declare unending war – by land, by sea, by ship, by sword, by me!'

▶ This Greek armour shows the head of a gorgon, a monster with hair of living snakes. Her gaze could turn people to stone.

When Aristophanes was writing his comedies, Athens was in the middle of a long war against Sparta. Every summer, the Spartans invaded the land around Athens and burned the growing crops. The Athenian farmers took refuge in the city. From its high walls, they watched their fields burn.

Aristophanes used his comedies to call for an end to the war. In *The Acharnians*, he mocked the leading general, Lamachus, and showed how the Athenian farmers were sick of the war.

◀ This vase shows a Greek hero with a gorgon on his shield.

'I think about my farm, I long for peace.
I hate this city life. I want my village.
I'll heckle and clap and shout,
If anyone talks of anything but peace.' [33]

▲ These chorus actors play the role of warriors.

26

All of Aristophanes' plays are 'political'. This word comes from the Greek *polis*, meaning city-state. To someone living in Athens, like Aristophanes, politics simply meant anything to do with the way the city was run.

▼ Athenian citizens vote, watched by Athene, goddess of the city.

The Athenians lived in the world's first *democracy*, a word which means 'people power'. Every citizen had a say in the government of Athens. Citizens held regular meetings where every important issue was discussed and voted on.

'Here in Athens ... we do not say that a man that takes no interest in politics minds his own business. We say he has no business here at all.' 35

▼ In wartime, ordinary citizens put on helmets like this one and fought for their city.

Meetings voted on such issues as the war with Sparta. They were attended by around 5,000 citizens, but three times this number went to watch the theatre festivals. This meant that playwrights had the opportunity to speak to a huge audience of fellow citizens, and influence the way their city was run.

IVY WREATH

THE PRIZE-GIVING

At the end of the festival, a herald announces the winning playwright: 'The prize goes to Sophocles!' A great cheer goes up from the audience, but a few men hiss. As Sophocles steps forward to be crowned with a wreath of ivy, a loud cry is heard from the back: 'Aeschylus should have won!'

▶ The winning playwright is crowned with a wreath of ivy.

'When Sophocles won the prize, Aeschylus was so upset that he stayed only a little longer in Athens, before retiring in anger to Sicily, where he died.' [36]

▲ The winning playwright's ivy wreath.

Almost everything that the Greeks did, including writing plays, was a competition. Greek men competed for fame and honour, and to please the gods. Religious festivals included competitions in athletics, poetry and music. The gods were thought to enjoy watching them.

The winning play was chosen by ten ordinary citizens who had been selected by lottery. These judges wrote down their decisions on tablets, which were placed in an urn. Only five of these tablets were pulled out to decide the winner of the festival.

▶ Festivals included other competitions. Running races were very popular.

◄ Ivy wreaths decorate this play's scenery, as a reminder of the playwright's prize.

▼ This is all that remains of a whole street of monuments built to hold theatre prizes.

A prize was also awarded to the choregos, the rich man who had paid for the winning chorus. The choregos received a bronze 'tripod', which was a three-legged cauldron. He then built a grand marble monument to display his prize, in the street leading to the theatre.

If you visit Athens today, you can still see one of these monuments. It marks the victory of a choregos called Lysicrates, in 354 BC. Lysicrates became a choregos to win lasting fame. He would be pleased to know that his monument is still standing.

'I went in for first prize – and I lost, I came third to bungling oafs, Quite unfairly. The judges were fools.' 38

GLOSSARY

airs The manners of someone who is showing off.

ambassadors Officials sent abroad as representatives of their government.

Athenians People who come from Athens.

backdrop A painted scene at the back of a stage.

catcalls Shrill whistles people make to show that they dislike something.

citizen Someone with full rights as a member of a state, such as the right to vote or sit on a jury. In ancient Greece, women and slaves were not citizens.

democracy A type of government in which power is held by the people, who make decisions by voting.

drama The art of writing and presenting plays.

exaggerated Larger than normal.

farces Comic plays in which a series of unlikely events occur.

frenzy Wild excitement or fury.

gorgon The gorgons were three monstrous sisters in Greek myth. The most famous sister was called Medusa.

grotesque Monstrous, in a funny or repulsive way.

heckle Shout things out at an actor during a performance.

lyre An ancient stringed instrument like a small harp.

moral A lesson or meaning, often explained at the end of a play.

myths Traditional stories, often with supernatural characters.

overacted Played a role in an exaggerated, unbelievable way.

papyrus An Egyptian water plant used for making paper – a word which comes from 'papyrus'.

playwright The writer of a play.

plots The stories and events of a play.

political Concerned with the state or its government.

satyrs Creatures in myth with the ears and tail of a horse.

skene The building where the actors changed their costumes and masks. It was decorated and used as the backdrop to the action, giving us our word 'scenery'.

windbag Somebody who talks a lot, but says nothing of value.

FURTHER READING

BOOKS TO READ

Acting and Theatre by Cheryl Evans and Lucy Smith
(Usborne, 1992)

Athletes and Actors by Anita Garneri
(Heinemann, 1997)

Entertainment by Jacqueline Morley
(Watts, 1994)

Greek Theatre by Stewart Ross
(Wayland, 1996)

On Stage by Michael Pollard
(Merlion Publishers Ltd, 1993)

The Greeks by Susan Peach and Anne Millard
(Usborne, 1990)

SOURCES OF QUOTES

1. All quotes in the illustrated scroll come
   from comedies by Aristophanes.
2. Aristotle, *Poetics*.
3. Aristophanes, *Acharnians*.
4. Aristophanes, *Clouds*.
5. Euripides, *The Bacchae*.
6. Aristophanes, *Knights*.
7. Aristophanes, *Frogs*.
8. Xenophon, *The Symposium*.
9. Spoken by Aeschylus in Aristophanes,
   Frogs.
10. Spoken by the chorus in Euripides,
   Hippolytus.
11. Demosthenes, *On the False Embassy*.
12. Aristophanes, *Frogs*.
13. Xenophon, *The Symposium*.
14. Aristophanes, *Clouds*.
15. Aristophanes, *Birds*.
16. Aristophanes, *Acharnians*.
17. Euripides, *The Bacchae*.
18. Aristotle, *The Poetics*.
19. Aristophanes, *Festival Time*.
20. Plutarch, *Moralia*.
21. Aristophanes, *Peace*.
22. Aristophanes, *Acharnians*.
23. Sophocles, *King Oedipus*.
24. Sophocles, *King Oedipus*.
25. Aristophanes, *Frogs*.
26. Sophocles, *The Cyclops*.
27. Aristophanes, *Peace*.
28. Sophocles, *The Cyclops*.
29. Aristophanes, *Frogs*.
30. Aristophanes, *Peace*.
31. Aristophanes of Byzantium, quoted by
   E. G. Turner, introduction to
   Menander, The Girl from Samos
   (University of London, 1972).
32. Plutarch, *Moralia*.
33. Aristophanes, *Acharnians*.
34. Aristophanes, *Acharnians*.
35. Thucydides, *History of the
   Peloponnesian War*.
36. Plutarch, *Life of Cimon*.
37. Aristophanes, *Clouds*.
38. Aristophanes, *Clouds*.

INDEX

Numbers in bold refer to pictures and captions.